The **Sickle Cell Anemia** Update

Alvin and Virginia Silverstein and Laura Silverstein Nunn

Titles in the DISEASE UPDATE series:

The Asthma Update
0-7660-2482-2

The Diabetes Update
0-7660-2483-0

The Flu and Pneumonia Update
0-7660-2480-6

The Sickle Cell Anemia Update
0-7660-2479-2

The STDs Update
0-7660-2484-9

The Tuberculosis Update
0-7660-2481-4

DISEASE
UPDATE

The **Sickle Cell Anemia** Update

Alvin and Virginia Silverstein and Laura Silverstein Nunn

Enslow Publishers, Inc.
40 Industrial Road
Box 398
Berkeley Heights, NJ 07922
USA

http://www.enslow.com

Acknowledgment

The authors thank Richard A. Drachtman, M.D., Associate Professor of Pediatrics; Medical Director, Pediatric Hematology/Oncology; and Director, Comprehensive Sickle Cell Program at Robert Wood Johnson Medical School, for his careful reading of the manuscript and his many helpful comments and suggestions.

Library of Congress Cataloging-in-Publication Data

Silverstein, Alvin.
    The sickle cell anemia update / Alvin Silverstein, Virginia Silverstein and Laura Silverstein Nunn.
        p. cm. — (Disease update)
    Includes bibliographical references and index.
    ISBN-10: 0-7660-2479-2 (hardcover)
    1. Sickle cell anemia—Juvenile literature.   I. Silverstein, Virginia B.
II. Nunn, Laura Silverstein. III. Title. IV. Series.
    RC641.7.S5.S573 2006
    616.1'527—dc22

                              2005018727

ISBN-13: 978-0-7660-2479-3 (hardcover)

Printed in the United States of America

10 9 8 7 6 5 4 3 2

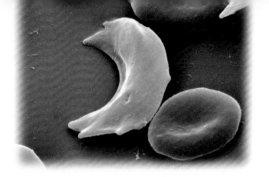

Contents

Sickle Cell Anemia

What is it?
A disease that affects the red blood cells. Some of the red blood cells become sickle-shaped. These sickle cells become stiff and pile up, blocking small blood vessels. Then body cells do not get enough oxygen.

Who gets it?
Mainly Africans and African Americans, but it is also found in people from the Mediterranean, the Caribbean, the Middle East, India, and Southeast Asia. It usually appears in childhood but may not cause symptoms until later.

How do you get it?
By inheriting it from your parents. It is not contagious and is not spread by germs.

What are the symptoms?
Tiredness, jaundice (yellowing of the skin and eyes), painfully swollen hands and feet, enlarged spleen, pains in the joints, frequent colds and other infections, slowed growth, and periods of intense pain.

How is it treated?
Daily penicillin and vaccination against pneumonia may help to protect children with sickle cell anemia from dangerous infections. Painkillers and drinking lots of fluids help to ease periods of intense pain. Drugs may prevent the formation of sickle cells. Blood transfusions may prevent stroke.

How can it be prevented?
Programs for screening newborns can identify people at risk for sickle cell disease to help prevent serious symptoms; screening and counseling can help in family planning.

Tionne Watkins, also known as T-Boz, became famous with her popular music group, TLC. Tionne is the national spokesperson for the Sickle Cell Disease Association of America. She is joined by fellow group member Lisa "Left Eye" Lopes (right) as they announce "Dime a Download," a music website that donates to the Sickle Cell fund.

1

A Crisis
in the Blood

THE NAME TIONNE WATKINS may not sound familiar to you. You may know her better by her nickname, T-Boz. T-Boz is the "T" in TLC, a popular music group in the 1990s that sold millions of records and earned four Grammy awards. T-Boz was twenty-one years old when she joined Lisa "Left Eye" Lopes and Rozanda "Chilli" Thomas in 1991 to form TLC. This was a dream come true for T-Boz. At just eight years old, T-Boz was diagnosed with sickle cell anemia. She was told that she would not be able to live out her dream of singing and dancing. But she refused to listen. Now she has accomplished more than anyone said would be possible.

As a teenager, T-Boz was determined not to let sickle cell anemia control her life. She was going to try to make the best of it. Positive attitude is the key, she believes. It isn't always easy, though. There are times when she has really bad days. "Sickle cell is very excruciating pain," T-Boz says. "It feels like somebody is stabbing you over and over again. There are sharp pains in my legs, where I can't walk. Sometimes I have to learn to walk all over again."

In 1996, T-Boz decided to go public about her condition. She also became the national spokesperson for the Sickle Cell Disease Association of America (SCDAA). As spokesperson, T-Boz educates people about the disease and helps raise money for sickle cell research. She also tells people about the importance of having a positive attitude, even when times are tough.

For T-Boz, her treatment involves eating lots of fruits and vegetables, exercising regularly, taking vitamins, including a daily dose of folic acid. (Folic acid helps to make more red blood cells.) T-Boz still has really bad days from time to time. Sometimes it gets so bad, she has to go to the hospital. There she receives pain medication and breathes through an oxygen mask to help her recover. Drinking plenty of fluids helps, too.

In 2000, TLC had to cancel two shows because of her illness. In 2002, her condition became so severe that she spent four months in the hospital.

Still, T-Boz refuses to let her condition bring her down. In 2000, T-Boz gave birth to her daughter, Chase. She calls Chase her "miracle baby" because she was told she couldn't have children. (Sickle cell anemia can damage a person's organs, including the reproductive organs.) In 2005, T-Boz opened a clothing store she named after her daughter, called Chase's Closet. In addition, she and Rozanda "Chilli" Thomas did a reality TV show, called *R U the Girl*, which gave the winner a chance to record a song with TLC.

What Is Anemia?

Sickle cell disease is often called sickle cell anemia because *anemia* is a typical effect of the disease. Anemia is a serious loss of red blood cells. Not enough red blood cells means not enough oxygen is getting to the body's cells. A person who is anemic may feel faint, dizzy, or drowsy.

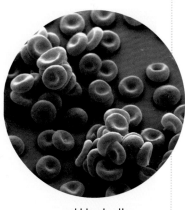

red blood cells

T-Boz knows how difficult it is to live with sickle cell anemia. But she refuses to give up hope and she tells others to do the same. The best way for people to deal with the disease she says, is to educate themselves.[1]

Sickle cell anemia is a blood disease. Sometimes the red blood cells change from their normal, round shape to a long, curved shape that looks like the blade of a sickle. (A sickle is a garden tool used to cut grass or grain.) That is how the disease got its name.

Sickle cell anemia is a blood disease. Sometimes the red blood cells change from their normal, round shape to a long, curved shape that looks like the blade of a sickle. That is how the disease got its name.

People with sickle cell anemia often have painful crises, or episodes of intense pain. These pain crises are caused by the formation of sickle cells, which pile up and block the flow of blood through the body. Sometimes the pain becomes so unbearable that people with sickle cell anemia have to go to the hospital.

Sickle cell anemia affects millions of people all over the world. It is most common in people whose families come from parts of Africa. But it also occurs in South America, Central America, Cuba, Saudi Arabia, India, and Mediterranean countries (such as Spain, Portugal, Turkey, Greece, and Italy). In the United States, sickle cell anemia affects about 72,000 people. Most of them are African Americans, but the disease can also affect other races.[2]

Sickle cell anemia is a chronic disease. *Chronic* means ongoing. People with the disease have to live with it for the rest of their lives. Before the 1970s, the outlook for sickle cell patients was not very good. It was not uncommon for children born with the disease to die at an early age because of complications. Many patients were not expected to live past their twenties. These days, however, early detection and better treatments have made it possible for children with sickle cell anemia to grow up to live longer, more productive lives.

> Sickle cell anemia is a chronic disease. People with the disease have to live with it for the rest of their lives.

In 1904, Walter Clement Noel traveled from Grenada to New York, and then to Chicago to attend dental school. Later that year, doctors diagnosed him with a type of anemia. In 1910, Dr. James Herrick wrote about Noel's symptoms in a medical journal. This was the first publication on the new condition, which was later named sickle cell anemia.

2

Sickle Cell Anemia in History

IN SEPTEMBER 1904, Walter Clement Noel, a twenty-year-old man from the West Indian island of Grenada, boarded a ship headed for the United States. He wanted to become a dentist and get his education at the Chicago College of Dental Surgery. During the voyage, Noel noticed a sore on his ankle, which became quite painful. When the ship docked in New York, Noel decided to go to a doctor, who gave him iodine to heal his wound. He then continued his journey to Chicago, where he became a dental student.

Near the end of November, Noel developed a serious chest infection. For a while, he suffered through his symptoms. The day after Christmas, though, he was feeling weak and dizzy, and went to the Presbyterian Hospital in Chicago. There Dr. Ernest E. Irons, a young hospital intern, took Noel's medical history and gave him a routine physical exam. He also took blood and urine samples. When Dr. Irons examined the blood sample, he noticed that some of the red blood cells looked strange, like nothing he had ever seen before. Dr. Irons then informed the attending physician on duty, heart specialist Dr. James Herrick, about his unusual findings.

Dr. Herrick listened to Noel's complaints of shortness of breath, heart palpitations, constant coughing, and aches and pains in his muscles. Noel also felt tired all the time, had headaches, bouts of dizziness, and he had sores on his legs. He told the doctor that he had had many of these symptoms since he was about ten years old. After writing down these symptoms, Dr. Herrick took another sample of Noel's blood and looked at it under a microscope. He thought that the patient had a kind of anemia, a serious loss of red blood cells. But this was not like any anemia he had seen before. To his surprise, many of the red blood cells had an odd shape. They were not tiny and round like red blood cells were supposed to be. They were long and curved, like

Dr. Ernest E. Irons, shown here in a 1940 photo, treated Walter Noel in 1904. Dr. Irons noticed that Noel's red blood cells looked strange. These oddly shaped red blood cells were later named "sickle cells."

crescents or sickles. Dr. Irons drew a rough sketch of these strange-looking red blood cells—the first pictures of sickle cells.

Dr. Herrick spent the next few years caring for his patient as best as he could, while studying this strange disease. Noel had to be treated in a hospital a number of times, but he still managed to finish his dental training. He went back home to Grenada in 1907 and set up a dental practice. However, Noel died from chest problems resulting from the disease at the age of thirty-two.

In 1910, Dr. Herrick reported his observations of Walter Clement Noel's unusual case in the scientific journal *Archives of Internal Medicine.* He became the first person to publish a medical report on the new condition that was later named sickle cell anemia.[1]

A New Disease

After Dr. Herrick published his report, other doctors observed patients with similar symptoms. A second case of unusual anemia with sickle-shaped cells was reported in 1911, a third case in 1915, and a fourth in 1922. All these new cases seemed to fit a definite pattern: Many patients had an African ancestry, and the disease appeared to be hereditary, as it affected parents as well as their children. As a number of other new cases continued to trickle in, doctors became desperate to uncover the mysteries of this new illness.

The term *sickle cell anemia* was first used in 1922, by Verne Mason, a doctor at Johns Hopkins Hospital in Baltimore, Maryland. After studying the first four case reports of this new disease, Mason noted similarities among the patients. Among them, he pointed out that they were all of African origin. This observation may have started the popular misconception that the disease affected only those with African ancestry.

The term *sickle cell anemia* was first used in 1922, by Verne Mason, a doctor at Johns Hopkins Hospital in Baltimore, Maryland.

In 1923, John Huck, an instructor at the Johns Hopkins University Medical School, became one of the first people to study heredity's role in sickle cell anemia. Huck studied information from two families. He concluded that sickle cell anemia is an inherited condition.

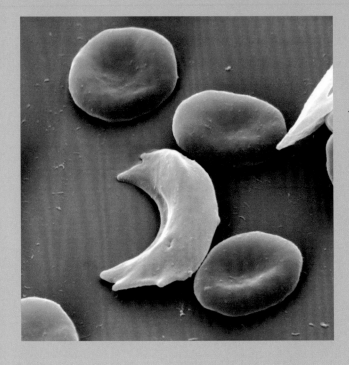

This microscopic view of red blood cells shows a sickle cell in the center. When the cells are sickled, they can become sticky and clump together. Then they can clog the blood vessels and cause pain and damage to the body's tissues.

In 1933, Dr. Lemuel W. Diggs, professor at the University of Tennessee College of Medicine in Memphis, explained that not all people who can form sickle cells get the disease. Those with sickle cell anemia have periods when many red blood cells "sickle," and they often experience unbearable pain. There are also people who have inherited a tendency to form sickle cells from one parent but not from the other. They are said to have the sickle cell trait. These people rarely develop symptoms because they do not have enough sickled cells to have an effect on the body. People with the sickle cell trait can live long, productive lives without any harmful effects of the disease.

Right Time, Right Place

In 1945, two Nobel-prize winners, Dr. William B. Castle, an expert on anemias, and Dr. Linus Pauling, a well-known chemist, took a train ride together and happened to talk about sickle cell anemia. Castle told Pauling about how the cells in sickle cell patients sickled more when oxygen levels were low. Pauling thought that hemoglobin, a chemical in red blood cells that carries oxygen, might be the key to the sickling problem.

Sickle Cell Goes On

Researchers have learned that people with the sickle cell trait, not the illness itself, seem to be protected against a deadly disease called malaria. Malaria is caused by a parasite that lives inside red blood cells. The parasite is carried by certain mosquitoes found in the tropics, especially Africa. These mosquitoes can pass the disease to people through their bite. Scientists have found that people with the sickle cell trait are more likely to survive malaria outbreaks than average people, or even those with sickle cell disease. As a result, the sickle cell trait has survived through the years, passing from one generation to the next.

Fascinated by the conversation with Dr. Castle, Dr. Pauling, along with his colleagues, did further research on sickle cell anemia. They found that an abnormal form of hemoglobin was indeed causing red blood cells to sickle. When the cells change their shape, they become sticky and clump together. Some of these abnormal blood cells are destroyed in the spleen, an organ that filters the blood for harmful substances. When red blood cells are destroyed, their total number drops. This causes anemia. Other sickle cells clog up the blood vessels, causing damage and pain to surrounding tissues, which are no longer receiving enough oxygen.

Soon Dr. Pauling was able to determine which people had the sickle cell trait and which had sickle cell anemia. The blood of people with the sickle cell trait contains a mixture of normal and abnormal hemoglobin. Dr. Pauling used a technique called electrophoresis to separate the two types of hemoglobin. A small sample of blood was placed on a gel-coated microscope slide. It was then placed in an electric field, and the different chemicals in the mixture moved along the slide at different speeds, forming separate spots. Once the hemoglobins were separated, Dr. Pauling was able to test for sickle hemoglobin.

A Key Difference

In 1956, another scientist, Dr. Vernon Ingram, used Dr. Pauling's tests to find the key difference between normal and abnormal hemoglobin. Like other proteins, hemoglobin is made up of chains of smaller chemical building blocks, called amino acids. These chains are folded and looped in a complicated structure. Dr. Ingram used chemicals to break some of the bonds in

Dr. Linus Pauling, shown here in a 1957 photo, invented a test for sickle cell anemia.

the hemoglobin molecule. This treatment turned the molecule into a mixture of shorter amino acid chains. By separating these pieces and sorting them out, it was possible to work out a map of the protein's structure. After comparing a normal hemoglobin molecule to an abnormal one, Dr. Ingram discovered that the two proteins had different amino acids in one spot on the chain. That single tiny change in the hemoglobin molecule seemed to be the cause of the sickling. It seems amazing that such a small difference could cause so many harmful effects in the body. Sickle cell anemia was the first hereditary disease for which the chemical change that caused it was known.

3

What Is Sickle Cell Anemia?

Sixteen-year-old Clifton Ray Kirkman likes to keep busy, both at school and in the community. Sometimes his life seems like a juggling act. Clifton is a member of the high school debate team. He also belongs to the high school choir group, which tours colleges around the country. He was especially proud when he was able to sing in Martin Luther King, Jr.'s church in Georgia during one of his tours. Clifton is also a member of three other choirs outside of school, which requires him to practice four nights a week. If that isn't enough to keep him busy, he is also the youth director of a young adult community choir of over fifty kids. What makes all this even more amazing is that Clifton suffers from sickle cell anemia.

Clifton was diagnosed with sickle cell anemia when he was only eighteen months old. He had been limping all day, and his leg seemed swollen. That night, Clifton's mother, Connie, brought him to the hospital, where they ran some tests. That is when they found out that Clifton had sickle cell anemia. Both Connie and her husband carry the sickle cell trait, so Connie had known this could happen. "I had always wanted to have a large family," says Connie, "but decided differently when I discovered we both had the trait." Clifton's sister, Jazmine, has the sickle cell trait, but she does not have the illness.

Clifton has been in and out of hospitals throughout his life. Sometimes his condition brings him unbearable pain. Often it comes on suddenly. It may last for a few minutes or as long as a week or two. He has also had a number of health problems related to his condition, including gall bladder problems and jaundice (yellowing of the eyes and skin). In some cases, surgery was needed to correct these problems. Every month, Clifton receives a blood transfusion to replace the sickle cells in his blood with normal red cells that will not clump up and clog the blood vessels. This treatment helps to ease his pain crises. Through it all, Clifton is still able to stay

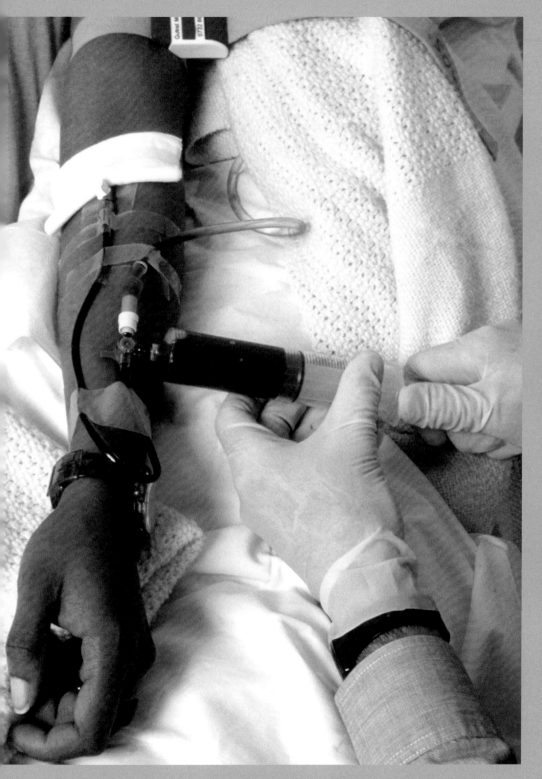

A patient receives a blood transfusion to treat her sickle cell anemia.

active and keep doing all his activities. Connie raised her son to believe that "he can do whatever he wants to do regardless of the illness."[1]

An Inherited Disease

Sickle cell anemia is not caused by a germ. People cannot "catch" the disease from someone who has it, the way they would a cold. Sickle cell anemia is hereditary. That means that the disease can be passed from parents to their children through their genes. Genes are chemicals that carry information determining a person's traits, such as curly hair, brown eyes, or big feet. In sickle cell anemia, a change in a gene causes red blood cells to change their shape—from soft, round cells that

> Sickle cell anemia is not caused by a germ. People cannot "catch" the disease from someone who has it.

look like doughnuts to long, curved, stiff cells that look like sickles or crescents.

A person with sickle cell anemia has a faulty gene. This gene controls the formation of hemoglobin.

The Alphabets in Your Cells

Everything about you—the color of your hair, the shape of your nose, even your blood type—is determined by chemicals called genes. Genes contain very long chains of a chemical called DNA. DNA is made up of four kinds of building blocks, which spell out all the body's hereditary information the way the letters of the alphabet spell out, or put in "code," words and sentences. Your genetic code spells out everything that makes you who you are.

The genes direct the formation of proteins from simple chemical units called amino acids. There are about twenty different kinds of amino acids in human cells. They form their own "alphabet," "spelling out" proteins. Each time a cell divides, all of its genes are copied to make another set for the new cell. Sometimes mistakes are made in copying, resulting in changes in the proteins spelled out by the genes.

Hemoglobin is an iron-rich protein that gives blood its red color. It is found in all red blood cells. Hemoglobin carries oxygen from the lungs to the body cells. It also takes carbon dioxide waste from the body cells to the lungs. Hemoglobin picks up these gases very easily, but it also lets go of them easily. That is why it works so well in carrying these gases through the body.

A change in just *one* "letter" in the gene that forms

part of hemoglobin results in a dramatic change in how hemoglobin works. This one-letter change is what causes sickle cell anemia.

Normal hemoglobin is known as hemoglobin A, or Hb A. People with sickle cell anemia make a different kind, hemoglobin S (Hb S). A number of other changes in hemoglobin can also cause problems that lead to sickling, but Hb S is the most common. Hemoglobin S

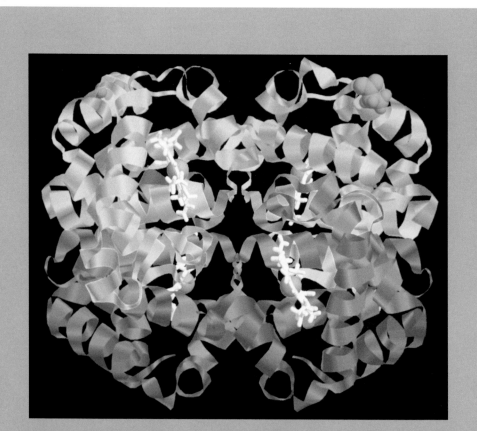

This is a computer graphic of normal hemoglobin, a protein in all red blood cells. Hemoglobin carries oxygen around the body. The white part of this graphic is heme, which connects to oxygen, carrying and releasing it through the body.

does not carry as much oxygen as Hb A. When there is not much oxygen in the blood, the hemoglobin S molecules stick together, forming stiff fibers. These fibers change the shape of the red blood cells into long, curved sickles.

Sickle cell anemia will develop only if a child inherits one sickle cell gene from the mother and one sickle cell gene from the father. People who inherit one normal hemoglobin gene and one faulty hemoglobin gene will carry the sickle cell trait. About 2 million Americans carry the sickle cell trait.[2]

People sometimes confuse sickle cell anemia with sickle cell trait. People with the sickle cell trait are carriers. Usually they do not have any symptoms or problems from the disease. Carriers do have sickle hemoglobin (Hb S), just like those with the disease. However, the amount is fairly low, about 30 percent Hb S. (A person with sickle cell anemia may have 80 percent or more Hb S.) The rest of a carrier's hemoglobin is normal (Hb A). This is enough to do a good job of carrying oxygen and carbon dioxide. Carriers should be aware, though, that their sickle cell trait can be passed on to their children.

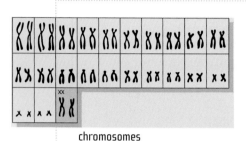
chromosomes

How Do We Inherit Our Traits?

Genes are lined up like beads on a necklace in structures called chromosomes. A complete set of chromosomes (forty-six in humans) is found in each body cell. Chromosomes come in pairs, and thus there are usually at least two genes for each trait, one inherited from each parent. Some genes are dominant—their effects are seen even if only one of the particular genes is present. Some genes are recessive—their effects appear only if two recessive genes are inherited, one from each parent. Sickle cell anemia is caused by a recessive gene for an abnormal form of hemoglobin. Therefore, this disease develops only when a person receives a sickle cell gene from *both* parents.

What's in Your Blood?

Because sickle cell anemia is a blood disease, it would help to understand it better if you know what goes on in your blood.

Blood is made up of four main parts: 1) plasma, 2) red blood cells, 3) white blood cells, and 4) platelets. Plasma is the liquid part of the blood—it makes up more than half of the blood. Red blood cells float in the plasma. They carry oxygen from the lungs to the body cells. White blood cells, which fight infection, and platelets, which are parts of cells that help stop bleeding, are also found in the plasma.

Blood can reach every part of your body through a system of tubes called blood vessels. The blood circulates around the body over and over again, which is why the heart and blood vessels are called the circulatory system. As blood leaves the heart, it flows through large blood vessels, called arteries. (So remember this: Arteries and Away from the heart both start with the letter A.) The arteries branch into smaller and smaller blood vessels. The tiniest blood vessels are called capillaries. They are so small that you could not see them without a microscope, and they have very thin walls.

Oxygen and food materials pass out through the capillary walls and into the body cells. Waste products from the cells pass into the bloodstream and are carried away. Blood returns to the heart through veins, and the process starts all over again, with every heartbeat. It takes less than a minute for the blood to circulate all around the body. This happens more than a thousand times a day.

Meanwhile, blood also flows through a smaller circle of blood vessels that leads from the heart to the lungs and back again. The air you inhale (breathe in) contains oxygen, a gas that body cells need to get energy from foods. It passes down into the lungs through branching tubes that look like an upside-down tree. The tiniest branches end in bubblelike air sacs. Like the capillaries, these air sacs have very thin walls. Each sac is surrounded by a net of capillaries. As blood flows by them, oxygen passes out through the walls of the air sacs and into the capillaries. The cells' waste products go from the capillaries into the air sacs, where they will be blown out the next time you exhale. One of the main waste products is a gas called carbon dioxide, which is formed when cells use food materials to produce energy.

Oxygen is carried in the blood mainly by the red blood cells. There are about 25 trillion red blood cells in an adult's body—more than 250 million in each drop of blood. Like most other body cells, they are microscopic, but they are actually wider than the openings inside the smallest capillaries. Red blood cells are soft and flexible. They can bend and twist to pass through the tiny capillaries. Eventually, though, they wear out. Red blood cells live for only about 120 days. The old, worn-out cells are broken down in the liver and spleen, and their chemicals are recycled.

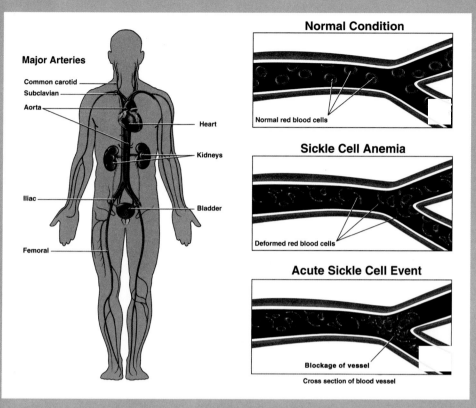

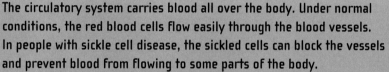

Major Arteries

Common carotid
Subclavian
Aorta
Heart
Kidneys
Iliac
Bladder
Femoral

Normal Condition

Normal red blood cells

Sickle Cell Anemia

Deformed red blood cells

Acute Sickle Cell Event

Blockage of vessel

Cross section of blood vessel

The circulatory system carries blood all over the body. Under normal conditions, the red blood cells flow easily through the blood vessels. In people with sickle cell disease, the sickled cells can block the vessels and prevent blood from flowing to some parts of the body.

Red blood cells are produced in the bone marrow, the spongy material that fills the spaces of the large bones. When the oxygen supply to the bone marrow is low, the bone marrow starts making more red blood cells. Each second, from 2 million to 10 million red blood cells in a person's body are destroyed. An equal number of new red blood cells are produced in the bone marrow to replace them.

The ABCs of Sickle Cell

(A) The person has Hb S instead of Hb A.

(B) Hb S does not hold as much oxygen as Hb A.

(C) With less oxygen, the red blood cells change into a sickle shape.

(D) The sickle-shaped cells clump together.

(E) Clumped cells block blood flow to tissues and organs, causing pain.

When Cells Sickle

The abnormal hemoglobin (Hb S) produced in people with sickle cell anemia cannot carry as much oxygen as normal hemoglobin. The lack of oxygen causes the red blood cells to change their shape from round and plump to long and curved, like the blade of a sickle. These sickle cells cannot bend and twist the way normal red blood cells can, and they cannot squeeze through the tiny capillaries. Instead, they become stiff and sticky. They get stuck in the narrow capillaries, and even in larger blood vessels. The sickle cells start to pile up in the blood vessels, clogging the openings. Fewer oxygen-carrying blood cells are able to get through, which leads to even more sickling.

People with sickle cell disease often develop anemia, a condition in which the number of red blood cells is below the normal level. Sickle cells are very brittle and tend to break apart easily. They have a very short life span—only 10 to 20 days—compared to the 120-day life span of normal red blood cells. So it is very difficult

People with anemia often feel weak or tired.

for the bone marrow to make enough red blood cell replacements. As a result, not enough oxygen can get to the body's tissues—which leads to even more sickling. People who are anemic often feel tired and weak.

Sickle-Cell Symptoms

Sickle-cell symptoms develop when the sickled cells plug up blood vessels. This prevents the oxygen-carrying blood from reaching important organs. Tissues near the blockage are starved of oxygen and nutrients.

The most common complaint in sickle cell anemia is the unbearable pain. People with sickle cell anemia have what they call pain crises, or episodes of intense pain. Pain crises are very unpredictable. The pain can develop in any organ or joint in the body, but the most common areas include the arms, legs, abdomen, chest, and back. The symptoms vary greatly from person to person and even within the same person. One person may have only one crisis a year, while another may have one every few weeks. Some people may go for months or years

> The most common complaint in sickle cell anemia is the unbearable pain. People with sickle cell anemia have what they call pain crises, or episodes of intense pain.

Why Does It Hurt?

When cells are damaged, or are not getting the oxygen and food materials they need, they call for help. They send out chemical alarm signals to tell the body they are in trouble. These signals are sent to the brain, which translates them into feelings of pain. The more cells that are damaged, the stronger the signals—and the more it hurts. You probably think of pain as a bad thing. It can be good for the body, though, if you take the warning and do something quickly to fix the problem.

without a crisis and then suddenly have one after another. A pain crisis usually lasts for a few hours to a few days, but sometimes it can last for weeks.

Sickle cell crises can have dangerous effects on the body. The lack of oxygen can damage important organs, such as the lungs, kidneys, and spleen. Sickle cells that cause narrowing and blockage in the blood vessels in the brain can cause a stroke. Brain cells that normally get oxygen and food materials from these blood vessels are starved. After just a few minutes without oxygen, they may begin to die. If many brain cells die, the person can no longer do the things those cells con-trolled—such as speaking or moving an arm or leg.

Fever is an early warning sign of illness. Young people with sickle cell anemia get sick more often.

How Important Is Your Spleen?

The spleen plays a very important role in protecting people from infections. It is packed with disease-fighting cells that protect the body from germs. Sickled cells may become trapped in the spleen, blocking tiny blood vessels and resulting in damage to the tissues they nourish. This damage makes it less able to fight infection. The blockage of spleen blood vessels may also cause the spleen to enlarge (become larger than normal), filling the whole abdominal area, as blood is trapped inside it. A hard, enlarged spleen is a common symptom in children with sickle cell anemia.

This kind of stroke occurs mainly in children. About 10 percent of children with sickle cell anemia have a stroke.[3] A stroke can lead to learning problems, and possibly even paralysis (loss of feeling or movement in a body part). Children with sickle cell anemia also get sick more often. They have a higher risk of developing serious illnesses, including pneumonia, meningitis, influenza, and hepatitis. Fever is an important early warning sign of illness. A fever of 101°F is a signal to call the doctor. If the fever rises to 103°F, the child should be rushed to the emergency room. Such a high fever may be caused by an infection in the blood. This can be very dangerous if it is not treated right away.

People with sickle cell anemia may develop jaundice, a yellowing of the skin and eyes. This condition is not harmful itself, but it is a sign of a problem in the blood. When jaundice develops along with other symptoms, including nausea, vomiting, and abdominal pain, it could be a sign of gall bladder problems.

Acute chest syndrome may develop as a result of infection or trapped sickled cells in blood vessels in the lungs. Symptoms include chest pain, coughing, difficulty breathing, and fever.

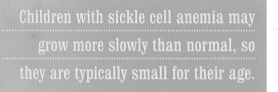
Children with sickle cell anemia may grow more slowly than normal, so they are typically small for their age.

Some people develop sores that do not heal. These sores are usually seen in adults. They are brought on by poor blood circulation and typically occur on the ankles. Poor circulation is also the cause of painful joints that affect older people with sickle cell anemia. The cutoff of the blood supply to the eyes can be so severe that it may even cause blindness.

A very common symptom in young children is the hand-foot syndrome. As tiny blood vessels become blocked by sickled cells, the hands and feet swell and become hot, red, and painful.

Children with sickle cell anemia may also grow more slowly than normal, so they are typically small for their age, with an underdeveloped body.

Usually people with sickle cell trait are free of symptoms of the disease. However, symptoms may develop under certain unusual conditions. For example, extreme stress, lack of oxygen, a high altitude (such as climbing a mountain), or dehydration (loss of fluids) after exercise might cause red blood cells to sickle. This does not mean that the person has developed the disease. Any symptoms, such as a bit of blood in the urine, will soon go away when the situation returns to normal.

Another Hemoglobin Disease: Thalassemia

Thalassemia, like sickle cell anemia, is an inherited disease that affects the hemoglobin in red blood cells. In thalassemia, there is not enough working hemoglobin to keep the body's organs supplied with oxygen. Anemia develops. Meanwhile, protein builds up inside the red blood cells. As a result, the cells become damaged and soon die, reducing the red blood cell supply.

Thalassemia usually affects people from areas surrounding the Mediterranean Sea, such as Italy, Greece, and the Middle East. In fact, its name comes from

Sickle Cell Anemia: Sign and Symptom Checklist

- Pain in joints, bones, chest, abdomen, arms, legs (may be sudden, chronic, and/or intense)
- Feeling very tired and weak (due to anemia)
- Shortness of breath
- Jaundice (yellowing of the skin and eyes)
- Fever
- Headache
- Blurry vision
- Slow-healing sores on lower legs
- Swelling of abdomen (due to enlarged spleen)

thalassa, the Greek word for "sea." The disease also occurs in Americans of Italian, Greek, Middle Eastern, Southern Asian, and African ancestry.

The most severe form of thalassemia is called thalassemia major, also known as Cooley's anemia, named after Dr. Thomas Cooley. It occurs when the genetic defect is inherited from both parents. Babies with this type may die if they are not properly treated. A milder form, called thalassemia intermedia, occurs when a severe form is inherited from one parent or the mild form is inherited from both. It is not usually fatal. The mildest form is called thalassemia minor. It occurs when the defect is inherited from only one parent. People with this form are carriers of the disease because they do not have any symptoms but may pass it on to their children. Thalassemia genes may also be combined with sickle cell genes, causing diseases with varying severity. The popular singer T-Boz Watkins, whose story was told in Chapter 1, was diagnosed as a child with sickle cell anemia. When she was in her twenties, however, new tests revealed that she actually had a combination of sickle cell anemia and thalassemia.

Symptoms of thalassemia are very much like sickle cell anemia. They may include tiredness, irritability, pale skin, poor appetite, and underdeveloped growth. A child may develop an enlarged heart, liver, and spleen.

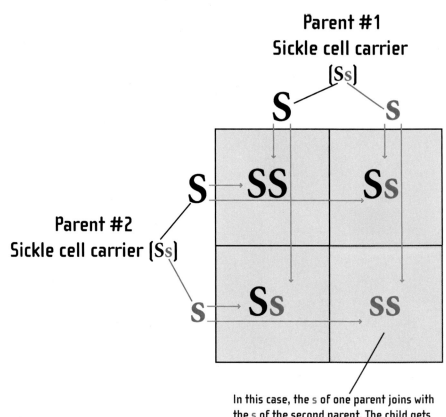

Parent #1
Sickle cell carrier
(Ss)

Parent #2
Sickle cell carrier (Ss)

In this case, the s of one parent joins with the s of the second parent. The child gets one s (sickle cell gene) from each parent. The child will have sickle cell disease.

S = normal hemoglobin gene

s = sickle cell gene

Each person has two genes that together determine whether they have sickle cell disease.

SS = gene pair of a person with normal hemoglobin

Ss = gene pair of a person with sickle cell trait (carrier)

ss = gene pair of a person with sickle cell disease

The four boxes above show the four possible outcomes for children of two parents who carry the sickle cell trait.

4

Detection and Treatment

When Olive Downer was pregnant, she knew there was a chance—a one in four chance— that her child could be born with sickle cell anemia. She and her husband were both carriers of the sickle cell trait. Only time would tell. After their daughter, Arianne, was born, the baby was tested for sickle cell anemia. The test came back negative, but the doctor told Olive that if her daughter had the disease, it would probably develop by the time she was a year old.

Arianne learned to walk at nine months old. She showed no symptoms of the disease and seemed to be healthy. When Arianne was one year old, her parents breathed a sigh of relief—she still seemed to be free of the disease. When Arianne was two years old, however, she suddenly had trouble walking. She complained that her hips hurt. She kept saying, "pain, pain . . ." as she pointed to her hips. Arianne was taken to the hospital, where they tested for sickle cell anemia again. This time the results were positive.

Olive worked with Arianne at home to get her back on her feet. With the help of a walker, Arianne eventually learned how to walk again.

During Arianne's early school years, she got frequent colds and a number of episodes of severe pain. Most of the time, Olive was able to care for Arianne at home, giving her over-the-counter medicine to ease the pain. However, about once or twice a year, the pain crises were so severe that she had to go to the hospital. There Arianne was hooked up to tubes dripping pain medicine into a vein in her arm until the pain went away.

As Arianne got older, the pain crises seemed to become more frequent and more severe. Sometimes the pain medication at home was not strong enough to get rid of the pain. When this happened, Arianne knew it was time to go to the hospital. From the ages of eleven to thirteen, her hospital stays averaged about fifteen times a year. On each visit, she had to stay from one to

Olive Downer, with her daughter, Arianne, and her son, Nathan. Arianne has sickle cell anemia.

two weeks, depending on what body part was affected. During some of the visits, Arianne received blood transfusions, which supplied her body with healthy red blood cells. This treatment helped to ease her pain.

At home, Olive does her best to help Arianne avoid pain crises. Arianne needs to dress warmly when it gets chilly outside because cold temperatures have been known to bring on a crisis. She also drinks plenty of water and gets plenty of rest.

Arianne realizes that she cannot do everything her friends can do because the pain crises are so unpredictable. But she remains hopeful about the future. She would like to be a veterinarian someday, travel around the world, and have at least one child.[1]

Thirty years ago, Arianne's hopes for the future would not have been very realistic. People with sickle cell anemia typically had short life spans. In the early 1970s, for example, someone with the disease could expect to live, on the average, to the age of eighteen.[2] Today, however, the majority of patients live past the age of fifty.[3] In fact, doctors at a major sickle cell health center in Atlanta, Georgia, are now following some patients well into their seventies.[4] Today, doctors know much more about the disease than they did years ago.

Accurate tests can give an early diagnosis, which is very important. Young children have a high risk for complications. Early treatment can not only ease the pain, but it can also help prevent dangerous health problems that might develop.

Blood Tests

A number of blood tests can be done to diagnose sickle cell anemia. One blood test is rather simple. It is used to screen the blood for abnormal hemoglobin (Hb S). A drop of blood is placed on a glass slide. The blood is mixed with a special chemical, which reduces the amount of oxygen it can hold. If there is Hb S in the blood, the lack of oxygen will change the shape of red blood cells into long, curved sickles. The sickle-shaped cells can be seen under a microscope. However, this test cannot tell the difference between people who have the disease and those who are carriers. In addition, this test does not work for babies because their blood does not contain enough Hb S to be picked up by the test.

Today, doctors know much more about sickle cell anemia than they did years ago. Accurate tests can give an early diagnosis, which is very important.

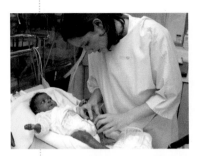

Protected at Birth

At birth, and even before birth, the blood contains mainly fetal hemoglobin. Fetal hemoglobin seems to somehow protect the baby from sickle cell anemia. By six months of age, however, this hemoglobin is replaced with adult hemoglobin. Sickle cell symptoms do not usually develop until after fetal hemoglobin is no longer in the blood.

There is a more effective blood test: hemoglobin electrophoresis. This test is widely used to confirm a diagnosis of sickle cell anemia. It is based on the test developed by Dr. Linus Pauling in the 1940s. This test is done by using an electric current to separate the different types of hemoglobin. Electrophoresis makes it possible to determine whether the patient has sickle cell trait or sickle cell anemia. If the person has sickle cell trait, about 20 to 40 percent of the hemoglobin will be Hb S. A person with the disease will have from 80 to 100 percent Hb S.[5] This test can also detect other hemoglobin blood disorders, such as thalassemia. The hemoglobin electrophoresis test can also be used to diagnose babies.

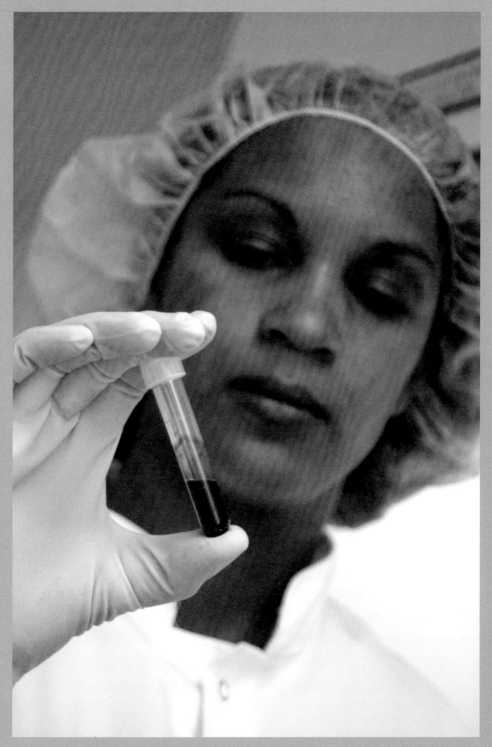

A number of blood tests are used to diagnose sickle cell anemia.

Blood tests can also provide additional information on the condition. For example, a complete blood count (CBC) gives the numbers of red blood cells as well as white blood cells. A low red blood cell (RBC) count is a sign of anemia. A high white blood cell (WBC) count shows that there is an infection in the body.

Controlling the Pain

The main concern for sickle cell patients is controlling the pain. Some people find that over-the-counter painkillers can help ease the pain. Applying a warm cloth or a heating pad to the affected area may also help. Doctors also recommend lots of fluids and plenty of rest. However, these methods do not always work. If the pain cannot be controlled at home, a trip to the hospital may be necessary. There, patients may need to be given stronger pain medication, usually intravenously (a hollow needle is placed into a vein in the skin, and the medication flows through the needle and into the vein).

Other treatment options are available. One promising approach is a drug called hydroxyurea. This drug may be given to patients over eighteen years old who have frequent pain crises and show early signs of damage to organs. Hydroxyurea works by increasing the

What Is Normal?

Men normally have more red blood cells (RBC) in their blood than women, and so they also have more hemoglobin (Hb). The averages for healthy adults are as follows:

- _Men_: RBC 5.4 million per microliter of blood
             Hb 14–18 grams per deciliter

- _Women_: RBC 4.8 million per microliter of blood
             Hb 12–16 grams per deciliter

(A microliter, or cubic millimeter, is about one-fiftieth of a drop of blood.)

In anemia, the number of red blood cells is about 17 percent less than the normal value, and there is also less hemoglobin:

- _Men_: RBC less than 4.5 million per microliter
             Hb less than 14 grams per deciliter

- _Women_: RBC less than 4 million per microliter
             Hb less than 12 grams per deciliter

amount of fetal hemoglobin in the blood. Remember, this is the special form of hemoglobin that seems to protect against sickling. It is produced in a fetus and for about six months after birth. By one year of age, the amount of fetal hemoglobin in the blood has dropped from 80 percent to only 1 to 2 percent. Hydroxyurea can act on the cells that produce hemoglobin and actually increase the production of fetal hemoglobin. Studies have shown that hydroxyurea can reduce the severity, as well as the number of pain crises, by 50 percent.[6] This drug cannot stop a pain crisis once it has started, however—it can only *prevent* one from coming on. It is not yet recommended for children. Studies on children seem to be promising, but the long-term effects of hydroxyurea are not yet known. Some health experts worry about possible effects it may have on a child's growth and development.

Blood Transfusions

Blood transfusions are often a very effective way to relieve the pain caused by sickle cell anemia. Blood from a healthy donor flows into the patient's body through a hollow needle inserted into a vein. The job of blood transfusions is to increase the number of healthy red blood cells. This keeps the percentage of sickle cells below the level that may cause a pain crisis.

However, transfusions are not recommended as a routine way of relieving a person's pain crises. Not only are they inconvenient, there are some dangers involved. Regular blood transfusions can lead to a buildup of iron in the body. Too much iron can damage the heart, liver,

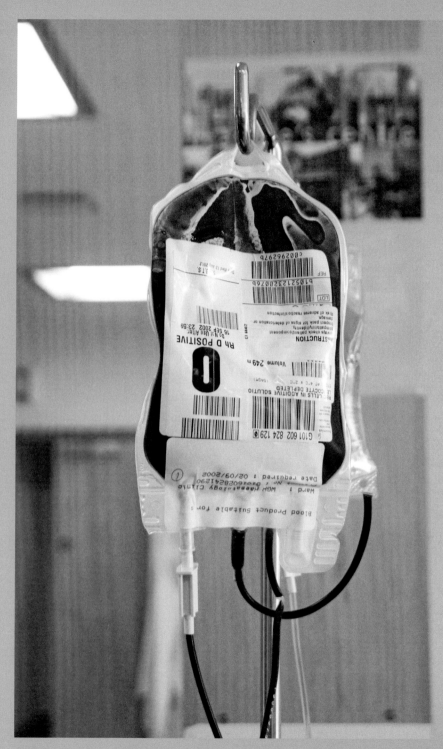

Blood transfusions deliver blood from a healthy donor to a person with sickle cell anemia. This helps increase the number of healthy red blood cells.

What Is Your Blood Type?

Do you know what your blood type is? This refers to the kind of proteins on the surface of your red blood cells. Everybody has a combination of many different surface proteins (antigens), which are inherited from their parents. One "blood group" is called ABO: Some people have an A protein (type A blood), others a B (type B), some have neither (type O), and some have both (type AB).

What happens if a person with type O blood receives a transfusion of type A blood or type B blood? The person's body would begin to produce antibodies against the "foreign" antigen. Antibodies are proteins that normally attack invading germs and protect the body from harm. They fit together with antigens like a lock and key. Antibodies against the A antigen, for example, would grab hold of the antigens on red blood cells from a type A transfusion. The red blood cells would be destroyed. This kind of reaction occurs whenever the blood for a transfusion is not correctly matched to the patient's blood, but it is even more likely in sickle cell patients.

and other important organs. Other problems may develop if the donor's blood does not match the patient's blood. "Mismatched" transfusions can result in a reaction that destroys a patient's red blood cells. This can lead to severe anemia and pain crises. The reaction may occur immediately, or up to several weeks later. Because of these possible problems, blood transfusions are given mainly to patients with a high risk for stroke or other complications.

Bone Marrow Transplants

Blood transfusions do not cure sickle cell disease. They provide the patient with healthy red blood cells, but after a while these new cells die off. (Remember, red blood cells live for only four months.) Meanwhile, the patient's bone marrow is making new red blood cells that contain sickle cell genes. Bone marrow transplants replace the cells that make red blood cells with healthy new blood-making cells that do not contain the sickle cell gene. So marrow transplants can actually cure sickle cell anemia in some patients. However, like any procedure, bone marrow transplants do involve some risks.

Bone marrow contains a lot of stem cells. These are immature cells that have the potential of developing into blood cells (white blood cells, red blood cells, and platelets). In a bone marrow transplant, the patient's bone marrow is destroyed with high doses of powerful drugs or radiation. It is then replaced with healthy bone marrow. The transplant is not a surgical procedure. It is done in the patient's hospital room. The patient receives the marrow through a needle, just like a blood transfusion. The new marrow is carried by the bloodstream to the cavities of the large bones, where it settles down and begins to produce healthy new blood cells.

The bone marrow for a transplant must be just as carefully matched to the patient's blood type as the blood for a transfusion. Otherwise, the body's own defenses, the immune system, could destroy the bone marrow.

The best chances of finding a bone marrow donor come from a close relative. Siblings have a 35 percent chance of being a match. The chances of getting a bone marrow match from an unrelated donor are not very likely. However, suitable matches may be found in various national and international bone marrow registries. These are lists of people who would be willing to donate bone marrow.

The procedure does not harm the donors. Only a portion of their bone marrow is removed, and their bodies soon replace it.

5

Prevention

In 2004, professional football player Terrell Owens was ranked the top wide receiver in the National Football League (NFL). That same year he was traded from the San Francisco 49ers to the Philadelphia Eagles. Playing for the Philadelphia Eagles, Owens made 77 receptions and 14 touchdown catches, more than any other NFL player that season.[1]

When Terrell Owens is on the field, it seems like nothing can stop him. He knows how to get the job done. Off the field, Owens is strong and determined as well, but he also has a big heart. In 1998, Owens lost his cousin to sickle cell anemia. She was only in her twenties. Every time he sees his cousin's son, he cannot help

Terrell Owens, a star NFL wide receiver, is very involved with the Sickle Cell Foundation. After losing a cousin to the disease, Owens works hard to tell people the importance of testing for the disease early in life.

but think of her and wonder what can be done to help other people with sickle cell disease. Owens has become a strong voice for the Sickle Cell Foundation, working to get the word out about the importance of testing for sickle cell. "A lot of people simply don't know whether they carry the sickle cell gene or not," says Owens, "and that can spell trouble . . . Get tested, and catch sickle cell before it can do damage."[2]

Although there is no cure for sickle cell anemia (other than transplants), there are things people can do

Stamp Out Sickle Cell

In September 2004, the U.S. Postal Service issued the Sickle Cell Disease Awareness postage stamp. The Sickle Cell Disease Association of America (SCDAA) worked with the U.S. Postal Service to design the stamp as part of a program aimed at calling attention to important health and social issues. They hope the stamp will lead to "a greater understanding of the seriousness of sickle cell disease and the thousands of lives it affects." It encourages early testing and treatment, and focuses attention on finding a cure. "The stamp will inspire hope in thousands of patients and their families throughout the world," commented SCDAA spokesperson T-Boz Watkins.[3]

to avoid serious health problems and reduce the number of pain crises.

Sickle Cell Screening

In 1987, the National Institutes of Health (NIH) recommended that all newborns be screened for sickle cell disease, regardless of their race.[4] Even though sickle cell disease is most common among African Americans, this blood disorder occurs in almost all racial and ethnic groups. In addition, it is not always easy to determine people's race or ethnic group correctly. Skin color and other characteristics vary greatly. Going by typical African, Asian, or Hispanic last names can be misleading as well, especially for those who have changed their names through marriage. So, if only African Americans are screened for sickle cell, others with the disease will be missed. Therefore, *everyone* should be screened.

> In 1987, the National Institutes of Health (NIH) recommended that all newborns be screened for sickle cell disease, regardless of their race.

Before the NIH's recommendations in 1987, fewer than fourteen states offered screening of newborns for sickle cell disease. By the early 2000s, however, newborns were routinely screened for sickle cell anemia in forty-four states, the District of Columbia, Puerto Rico, and the Virgin Islands. In the remaining six states, screening can be done by request.[5]

Sickle cell screening is performed along with the usual set of blood tests done on newborns. Screening has become highly specialized over the years. Computers can analyze a sample of blood for hundreds of different components. So the screening includes not only sickle cell testing, but also tests for a variety of hereditary conditions, including thalassemia and other hemoglobin disorders.

What Good Is Screening?

Over the years, people have questioned whether it is really necessary to screen for sickle cell anemia. After all, there is no cure. And there is no way of preventing the disease. However, studies have shown that newborn screening is very important in long-term survival. If a child is diagnosed with sickle cell disease at birth, daily doses of penicillin can be started right away. Infection is the most common cause of death in children with sickle cell anemia. Penicillin helps fight off the life-threatening infections before they develop.

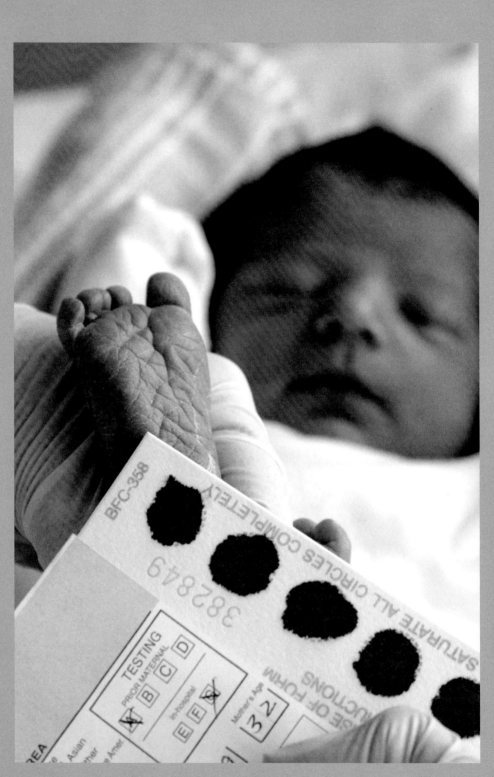

Sickle cell screening of newborn babies is performed along with other blood tests.

Doctors recommend that penicillin be taken daily until the child is five years old, when the body's immune system is stronger. This treatment seems to really work. Studies have shown that babies given penicillin every day had 84 percent fewer infections—and none died.[6] Vaccination against common diseases, including influenza (the flu) and pneumococcal pneumonia, also help protect the child's health.

Identifying the sickle cell trait—not just the disease—is also very important. As we discussed earlier, usually the sickle cell trait does not cause any trouble for the carrier. However, under certain conditions—too much stress, overexhaustion from exercise or sports, or being in low-oxygen altitudes (such as climbing a mountain)—red blood cells may start to sickle, resulting in sickle cell symptoms. Knowing whether they have the trait can help people avoid those special conditions, where problems could develop.

Genetic Counseling

Many people do not know whether or not they carry the sickle cell trait. But knowing their status can help prevent sickle cell disease in future generations. Genetic counseling can help people learn more about the

To Screen or Not to Screen?

Some people feel that genetic testing could lead to discrimination. People carrying genes that make them more likely to develop diseases such as sickle cell anemia or cancer might not be able to get health or life insurance, or they might not be allowed to take certain kinds of jobs. When sickle cell screening programs were first set up, in the 1970s, these fears were quite realistic. People with sickle cell disease were not allowed to be airplane pilots, for example. Even some students carrying the sickle cell *trait* were forced to leave the air force military academy. Since there were no effective treatments for sickle cell disease at the time, screening offered no real benefits other than giving carriers information to decide on whether to have children. And because the trait was most common among African Americans, many people thought screening programs were racist.

The situation has changed greatly since then. Effective treatments for the disease make it desirable for people to know whether they carry sickle cell genes. Federal laws and regulations, such as the Americans with Disabilities Act of 1990, provide some protection against discrimination in the workplace, and many states now have laws strictly regulating the use of genetic information for insurance and employment purposes.[7]

disease and the chances that their children will inherit their defective genes.

Genetic counseling usually involves a three-step process. First, the genetic counselor needs information on the family medical history. Are there any disorders in family members? Second, genetic tests may be ordered if the couple had not yet been screened for sickle cell trait. After examining the test results, the counselor will try to calculate the risks of passing on the disease to the couple's future children. Finally, the counselor must explain to the couple exactly what kind of genetic risks they face, what the odds are, and what choices they can make to avoid giving birth to a child with sickle cell disease. If the couple decides to take the risks, the genetic counselor will prepare them for what they can expect: the treatments, the costs, the emotional stress involved, and the likeliness of success.

The genetic counselor also talks to the couple about other options, if they both have sickle cell genes and do not want to take the chance that their future children will inherit the disease. One possibility is artificial insemination, often used to help people who are unable to have children. This treatment involves inserting the sex cells from a male donor (without the sickle cell

What Are the Odds?

If two carriers have children together, the chances of having a child with normal hemoglobin is 25 percent. The chances of having a child with sickle cell trait is 50 percent. And the chances of having a child with sickle cell anemia is 25 percent.

gene) into the female. Another option is choosing adoption.

Preventing Crises

Although the disease itself cannot be prevented, there are a number of things people can do to avoid symptoms or lessen the number of crises.

First of all, people with sickle cell anemia need to eat properly. With a balanced diet—including meat, poultry, or fish; grains; dairy products; fruits; and vegetables—the body has a better chance of fighting off any infections. Taking vitamins in addition to well-balanced meals is also very helpful. For example, folic acid supplements help the body make more red blood cells. Folic acid (a B vitamin) can also be found in leafy vegetables, mushrooms, fruit, and liver.

Drinking plenty of fluids is also very important. It is a good idea to drink some water or juice every hour. This keeps the blood flowing well, which prevents the sickle cells in the blood vessels from clumping. When people with sickle cell anemia do not get enough fluids, they become weak, which can bring on a crisis.

People with sickle cell anemia tire easily, so it is very important that they get plenty of rest. If they get tired in the middle of the afternoon, they should take a nap, even if only for a short time.

People with sickle cell anemia should exercise every day—as long as it is not too strenuous. Just walking can help keep the body in shape and healthy enough to prevent illnesses. Overdoing it and exercising to the point

Although the disease itself cannot be prevented, there are a number of things people can do to avoid symptoms or lessen the number of crises.

of exhaustion is not a good idea, since stress can bring on a crisis. Taking a rest now and then can help to keep from overdoing it.

Cold weather can be very difficult for people with sickle cell anemia. One of the ways the body usually

A healthy diet can help prevent sickle cell crises. Folic acid, a vitamin found in green leafy vegetables, mushrooms, and fruit, is especially important because it helps the body make more red blood cells.

deals with cold is by narrowing the blood vessels in the skin. This cuts down the loss of body heat. However, the reduced blood flow means less oxygen in these tissues. As a result, sickled cells may develop and plug the narrowed vessels, bringing on a pain crisis. So people with sickle cell anemia need to dress as warmly as possible when it is cold outside.

People with sickle cell anemia should stay away from places where the oxygen is low, since lack of oxygen can cause blood cells to sickle. It would not be a good idea to go scuba diving or hiking in the mountains. Flying in commercial airplanes is safe because they are completely pressurized, keeping a normal amount of oxygen in the air. However, flying in some military planes can be dangerous because they may not be pressurized and the oxygen level may be low.

It is very important to stay away from any kind of infection if possible. Since people with sickle cell anemia have a weakened immune system, even a simple cold may bring on a pain crisis. Pneumonia is one of the most common complications and is responsible for a large number of deaths of children with sickle cell anemia.

Most importantly, people need to know their own

People with sickle cell anemia should dress warmly when they are outdoors. Cold weather can narrow blood vessels, sending less oxygen to certain parts of the body. This can cause cells to sickle and plug the blood vessels.

personal "triggers"—things that bring on their pain crises. Write them down if necessary. Figuring out what can trigger a crisis, such as colds, swimming in a cool pool or the ocean, playing in the snow, or being stressed out or exhausted, can help people avoid what is making

To Do List

People who have sickle cell anemia should take care of themselves and see a doctor regularly. Here's a checklist of what to do to avoid problems:

- Eat a healthy diet. Take a daily dose of folic acid to help the body make new red blood cells.

- Drink lots of water every day.

- Get plenty of sleep.

- See a doctor regularly for checkups and treatment.

- See a dentist regularly to prevent loss of teeth and infections.

- Stay away from sick people.

- Learn about sickle cell disease and what signs of problems to look out for.

- Avoid overexertion (in exercise or sports), stress, and extremes of heat or cold.

- Avoid personal triggers.

them sick. T-Boz Watkins says that she and her mother gradually made a list of things that caused her crises. But even though she knew what to do, it was sometimes hard to stick to it. "When I was younger I didn't want to admit I had it [sickle cell anemia], so I went against the rules, and that really messed me up. I felt I didn't have to accept that something was wrong with me, that I could ignore it and I'd be fine. I wanted to be normal and to do what everyone else was doing. I'm not like that anymore, though. These days I'm careful to avoid doing things that cause crises."[8]

6

Sickle Cell Anemia and the Future

Throughout his childhood, Keone Penn was in and out of hospitals because of his severe sickle cell anemia. He had frequent pain crises, and at just five years old, he suffered a stroke. Keone had to receive regular blood transfusions to ease the pain. But eventually, even the blood transfusions were no longer helpful.

Doctors thought that Keone was a good candidate for a bone marrow transplant. They tested his half-sister, hoping that she would be a possible donor, but her blood was not a good match to Keone's. Then they tried to find an unrelated bone marrow donor, but they were unsuccessful. Keone's doctor, Dr. Andrew Yeager, wanted to try a new approach—doing a transplant with cord blood from an unrelated donor. Cord blood transplants had been used to save many leukemia patients, but the procedure had never been tried for sickle cell disease.

Cord blood comes from the umbilical cord after childbirth. It is full of stem cells, immature cells that can become any kind of blood cell. Cord blood transplants do not have to be a perfect match to work, as in bone marrow transplants. This provides more options for people who cannot find marrow donors, as in Keone's case.

On December 11, 1998, twelve-year-old Keone Penn became the first person to receive a cord blood transplant from an unrelated donor to treat sickle cell disease. Recovery turned out to be a long and difficult process. Keone wound up back in the hospital a number of times for various problems including fevers, diarrhea, and loss of appetite. Nine months after the transplant, the new immune system that had developed from the transplanted cord blood cells started to attack Keone's own body cells. This often happens in transplants: The transplanted cells identify the body cells as "foreign" and attack them as if they were an enemy. This

Keone Penn, left, received a cord blood stem cell transplant to treat his sickle cell anemia. Here he visits Capitol Hill to meet Dr. Pablo Rubinstein from the New York Blood Center.

reaction (known as graft-versus-host disease, or GVHD) caused inflammation (swelling) in Keone's liver and intestines. He was given strong drugs to prevent further damage to his body's organs.

One year after the transplant, Keone was declared "cured" of sickle cell disease. His cord blood cells were finally working properly. There were no signs of sickle cells in his body, and he no longer had pain crises. He no longer needed blood transfusions to protect him from stroke.[1] In 2004, Keone graduated from high school and entered culinary school to train as a chef.[2] "My stem cell transplant was not easy," Keone says, "but I thank God that I'm still here. . . . Sickle cell is now a part of my past. . . . Cord blood saved my life."[3]

Cord Blood Transplants

The cord blood that helps sickle cell anemia patients used to be just thrown away. Years ago, the placenta and umbilical cord that pass out of the mother's body after the birth of a baby were routinely treated as "medical waste"—garbage. Now doctors realize how valuable it is.

In cord blood transplants, the donor is not harmed in any way. Blood is taken from the umbilical cord and placenta right after birth. (The stem cells would break down within twenty-four hours.) The blood is then frozen and stored until it is needed. The stem cells in cord blood do not react to "foreign" antigens because the immune system of a newborn baby is not fully developed yet. Patients who receive cord blood transplants are thus much less likely to develop graft-versus-host disease. (In some cases it can happen, though, as it did with Keone.) Cord blood is also less likely to transmit infections than bone marrow from a donor who had been exposed to a variety of disease-causing germs. Another benefit is that the young stem cells have an enormous potential for growth and multiply quickly in the patient's bone marrow. In

Cord blood can be used to cure sickle cell disease. But it is not a treatment that can be used for everyone.

addition, only a few ounces of cord blood are needed for the transplant, whereas as much as a quart or more is needed for bone marrow transplants.

Thus, cord blood can be used to cure sickle cell disease. But it is not a treatment that can be used for everyone, because of the limited supply and the many risks involved. At present it is used only for severe cases, such as Keone's—especially when there is a risk of stroke.

Inflammation Causes Trouble

You may have noticed that when you have a splinter in your finger, if it is not taken out promptly, the skin around the splinter gets red and swollen and feels hot.

This is a normal body reaction called inflammation. It helps to fight germs that could cause infection. Inflammation occurs when damaged cells send special chemicals into the bloodstream. Recently researchers have been discovering that inflammation is involved in many serious diseases, including heart disease, diabetes, and asthma. In 2004, it was reported that inflammation may also play an important role in sickle cell disease.

Researchers have found that a chemical called tissue factor (TF) helps blood to clot (form a solid lump).

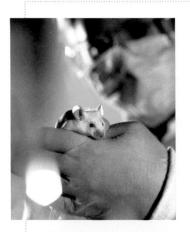

Mouse Models

Working with experimental animals allows medical researchers to learn more about human diseases and develop new tests and treatments. However, animals do not normally suffer from sickle cell disease. In 1997, scientists successfully transferred *human* sickle cell genes to mice, producing a "mouse model" of the disease. There are two kinds of these special mice. One makes both sickle hemoglobin and fetal hemoglobin, and has mild symptoms. The other makes only sickle hemoglobin and has symptoms of severe sickle cell disease.

When a blood vessel is cut, the damaged cells make TF. It results in a clot that helps to plug up the hole and

Clots inside blood vessels can block blood flow. This can cause a heart attack or a stroke.

stop the bleeding. But clots *inside* blood vessels can block blood flow. This can cause a heart attack or a stroke. People with sickle cell disease also produce higher-than-normal amounts of TF, especially during a pain crisis. In experiments on mice, researchers have found that drugs called statins can lower the amount of TF in the blood and prevent sickle cells from forming. Statins are used to help lower the risk of heart disease. They may also be helpful in treating sickle cell anemia patients.[4]

Another recent finding fits into the growing idea that inflammation and blood clotting are involved in sickle cell crises. The faulty hemoglobin gene also produces changes in the outer "wrapper" of red blood cells. Researchers at the University of North Carolina have found a protein on the surface of red blood cells in sickle cell patients that makes the blood cells stick to the blood vessel walls. This can lead to a sickle cell crisis. "It was previously thought that sickle red blood cells lodged in blood vessels because they're sickle-shaped,

Just Add Water

The red blood cells of people with sickle cell disease break down so quickly that the bone marrow is constantly racing to produce new ones to replace them. Some of the new red blood cells pass into the bloodstream in a not-quite-finished form. These immature red cells tend to lose water. As they dry out, their hemoglobin molecules get crowded together and are more likely to stick together. The cells become stiff and lose their ability to bend easily. That makes them bunch up in narrow blood vessels, leading to pain crises. Now researchers are studying chemicals that help to keep more water in the red blood cells, as possible drugs for treating sickle cell anemia.[5]

more rigid and just became physically stuck," says Dr. Julia Brittain, a coauthor of the study. But actually, she notes, "sickle red blood cells are simply stickier."[6] Drugs that block the "sticky" protein have already been developed and are being tested on sickle cell patients.

Researchers are also looking into another part of the inflammation puzzle: a chemical called nitric oxide. This chemical is produced naturally in the body and helps repair injured blood vessels. Nitric oxide works to stop blood clotting and keeps white blood cells from sticking to the blood vessel walls, thus decreasing inflammation. It also makes the blood vessel walls relax, widening the channel through which blood can flow. Sickle cell patients, however, tend to have less nitric oxide than normal. Researchers at Massachusetts General Hospital found that when nitric oxide gas was added to samples of blood from sickle cell patients, it caused their hemoglobin to hold onto oxygen more tightly. Then they had volunteers breathe air with small amounts of nitric oxide. In eight out of nine volunteers with sickle cell disease, the red blood cells held onto oxygen more tightly for at least an hour after they breathed the gas. Tests are underway to determine if breathing nitric oxide can help reduce symptoms in sickle cell patients.[7] Meanwhile, other researchers are studying the effects of drugs that help to increase nitric oxide production and block its destruction—including statins.[8]

Gene Therapy: Closing In on a Cure

Bone marrow or cord blood transplants can cure sickle cell disease: The patient no longer has to take medicine to prevent crises. But these treatments introduce "foreign" cells into the body, and they can lead to problems on their own. Researchers are working on a better way

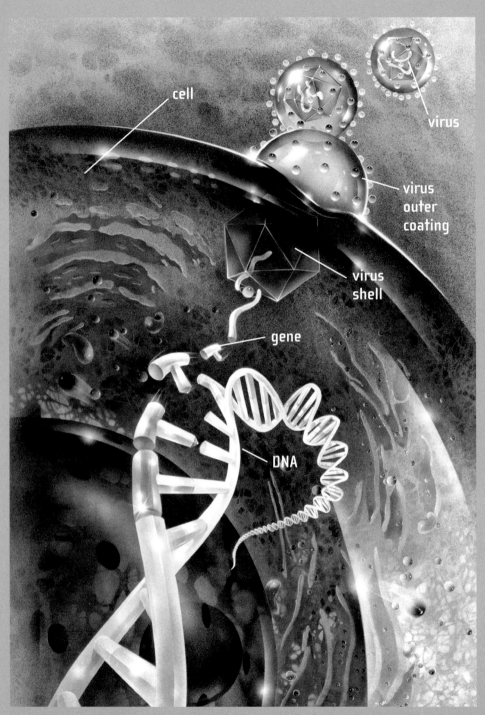

cell

virus

virus
outer
coating

virus
shell

gene

DNA

This artwork depicts gene therapy. A virus (red) is placing its genes (orange) into a strand of DNA (blue) inside a cell. Scientists can manipulate a virus's genetic material so that it places healthy genes into cells to correct genetic disorders.

to cure sickle cell disease—changing the genes of the patient's own cells so that the blood will not sickle. Unlike transplants, this can be done *without* destroying the patient's own blood-forming cells first.

In 2001, researchers at Harvard Medical School and Massachusetts Institute of Technology (MIT) announced that they had used gene therapy to cure sickle cell disease in mice. First they removed some of the mice's bone marrow. They treated the bone marrow cells with a combination of fetal hemoglobin genes and genes from a virus to help carry them into the cells. Meanwhile, they destroyed the bone marrow of two groups of normal mice. They injected the gene-treated bone marrow into one group and the untreated sickle-cell bone marrow into the other. The mice that received untreated sickle-cell bone marrow developed sickle cell disease, but those that received gene-treated bone marrow did not.[9]

In 2003, another group took the study one step further. Instead of giving the treated bone marrow cells to normal mice whose own marrow had been destroyed, they injected them into mice with sickle cell disease. The new bone marrow cells produced enough fetal hemoglobin to prevent sickle cell crises. (Just 1,000

SPOTLIGHT
Dedicated Researcher

As a child growing up in Wisconsin, Betty Pace learned firsthand how devastating sickle cell anemia can be. She watched helplessly while a close friend went through one crisis after another and finally died. At the time, around 1970, treatments were not very effective, and the life expectancy of people with sickle cell disease was only eighteen years. While still in junior high, Betty decided to dedicate her life to finding a cure.

After completing her studies in medical school, Betty worked as a pediatrician and also did research on sickle cell disease. Gradually she devoted more and more of her time to research. She is now an Associate Professor at the University of Texas in Dallas and Associate Director of the Sickle Cell Research Center there. Her lab is working on several projects involving fetal hemoglobin. Although people normally stop making this form of hemoglobin at around six months of age, the gene for it still remains in their body cells. Betty Pace's group is trying to find ways to turn the fetal hemoglobin gene back on in sickle cell anemia patients. They are also trying to develop gene therapy to prevent the change from producing fetal hemoglobin to making the adult form in people with sickle cell disease. Either approach would keep the blood from sickling and prevent crises.

In 2004, *Popular Science* magazine named Betty Pace one of the "Brilliant 10" scientists in the United States.[11] For a movie of Dr. Pace answering questions at the opening of the Sickle Cell Research Center, go to the Web at <http://www.utdallas.edu/research/ibmst/multimedia/>.

corrected bone marrow cells were enough to do the job. Remember, there are *trillions* of red blood cells in your body.)[10] More studies will be needed before gene therapy can be used for human sickle cell patients.

* * * * *

With so many promising lines of research on sickle cell disease, it seems certain that better treatments and permanent cures will be available in the near future.

Questions and Answers

Can I catch sickle cell anemia from a friend who has it?
No, it is a hereditary disease and is not caused by germs.
But if *you* have a cold or flu, it would not be a good idea
to visit until you are all better. Your friend could catch
the germs from you, and infections can set off a painful
sickle cell crisis.

Is it called sickle cell disease or sickle cell anemia? Both
terms are used. One of the most common effects of this
disease is anemia, a shortage of oxygen-carrying red
blood cells.

**Both of my parents have the sickle cell trait. Does that
mean I am guaranteed to get sickle cell anemia?** Not
necessarily. Having two parents with the sickle cell trait
does not "guarantee" that you will get the disease. But it
does increase your risk of getting it. Actually, there is a
25 percent chance that you will get it and a 25 percent
chance that you won't have any sickle cell genes. But
there is a 50 percent chance that you will get the trait,
which can be passed down to your children.

How do I find out if I have the sickle cell trait? You take a
blood test. This test will check for sickle hemoglobin

and can also tell if you have genes for other hemoglobin disorders, such as thalassemia.

My little sister just got diagnosed with sickle cell anemia. Does that mean I have it, too? Not necessarily—and if you haven't had any symptoms by now, it's likely that you don't have the disease. But there's a good chance that you do have sickle cell trait, so it would be a good idea to have a blood test.

If I have sickle cell trait, does that mean I'm sick? No. Usually sickle cell trait does not cause any health problems. But there may be some risk if you are in a situation where you are not getting enough oxygen— for example, if you climb a mountain or fly in an unpressurized airplane. Strenuous exercise in very hot weather could also be dangerous. Be sure to take breaks and drink a lot of fluids.

If I don't have sickle cell anemia, do I really need to find out if I have the sickle cell trait? If you want to have children, it would be a good idea. Then, if you marry someone who is also carrying the trait, you will know what you are facing and can make realistic plans for your family.

When we found out that my little sister has sickle cell disease, the doctor said she has to take penicillin every day, even when she isn't sick. Is that good for her? Yes, it may save her life! Children with sickle cell anemia can catch infections easily, especially pneumonia. Some have even died. Penicillin helps the body to fight germs before they have a chance to multiply and cause illness.

Sickle Cell Anemia Timeline

1910 .... Dr. James B. Herrick publishes the first medical report on sickle cell anemia.

1922 .... Dr. Verne Mason becomes the first to use the term *sickle cell anemia*.

1923 .... John Huck studies heredity's role in sickle cell anemia based on two families.

1933 .... Dr. Lemuel W. Diggs describes two forms of the disease: sickle cell anemia and sickle cell trait.

1945 .... Dr. Linus Pauling discovers that an abnormal form of hemoglobin was the cause of the sickling in sickle cell patients.

1956 .... Dr. Vernon Ingram discovers that the difference between normal and abnormal hemoglobin lies in a single amino acid.

1972 .... Congress passes the National Sickle Cell Anemia Control Act. It provides money from the government to fight sickle cell anemia.

1984 .... The University of Chicago Medical Center reports its first bone marrow transplant for sickle cell treatment.

1986 .... The National Heart and Lung Blood
Institute reports that daily doses of
penicillin are effective in preventing
serious infections in children.

1987 .... The National Institutes of
Health recommends widespread
newborn screening for sickle
cell anemia.

1998 .... The first unrelated donor cord
blood transplant is performed for
sickle cell anemia.

1998 .... The Food and Drug Administration
(FDA) approves hydroxyurea, the first
drug used to prevent pain crises in
adult patients with sickle cell anemia.

2001 .... Researchers, for the first time, correct
sickle cell anemia in mice using
gene therapy.

For More Information

American Sickle Cell Anemia Association
10300 Carnegie Avenue
East Office Building (EEb18)
Cleveland, Ohio 44106
(216) 229-8600
Web site: http://www.ascaa.org

Cooley's Anemia Foundation, Inc.
129-09 26th Avenue, #203
Flushing, NY 11354
(800) 522-7222
E-mail: info@cooleysanemia.org
Web site: http://www.thalassemia.org/

Information Center for Sickle Cell
and Thalassemic Disorders
(617) 768-8880
Web site: http://sickle.bwh.harvard.edu/

National Heart, Lung, and Blood Institute
Health Information Center
Attn: Web Site
P.O. Box 30105
Bethesda, MD 20824-0105
(301) 592-8573
E-mail: NHLBIinfo@nhlbi.nih.gov
Web site: http://www.nhlbi.nih.gov

Sickle Cell Disease Association of America
16 S. Calvert St., Suite 600
Baltimore, Maryland 21202
(800) 421-8453
E-mail: scdaa@sicklecelldisease.org
Web site: http://www.sicklecelldisease.org/

The Sickle Cell Information Center
P.O. Box 109
Grady Memorial Hospital
80 Jessie Hill Jr. Drive SE
Atlanta, GA 30303
(404) 616-3572
E-mail: aplatt@emory.edu
Web site: http://www.scinfo.org/

Chapter Notes

Chapter 1. A Crisis in the Blood

1. Tameka L. Hicks, "T-Boz: Fighting against the odds," *USA Weekend Magazine*, November 7, 2004, <http://www.usaweekend.com/04_issues/041107/041107t_boz.html> (April 5, 2005).

2. National Heart, Lung, and Blood Institute, "Who Gets Sickle Cell Anemia?" September 2003, <http://www.nhlbi.nih.gov/health/dci/Diseases/Sca/SCA_WhoIsAtRisk.html> (March 28, 2005).

Chapter 2. Sickle Cell Anemia in History

1. Todd L. Savitt, "The First Two Sickle Cell Anemia Patients in the Medical Literature—A Study in Contrasts," *The Brody School of Medicine at East Carolina University*, Fall 1998, <http://www.ecu.edu/medhum/newsletter/fall1998_p2.htm> (March 29, 2005).

Chapter 3. What Is Sickle Cell Anemia?

1. Carol Jachim, ed., "Spotlight on Life," *American Red Cross*, May 2003, <http://www.semredcross.org/bsv/spotlightonlife_ckirkman.pdf> (April 19, 2005).

2. National Heart, Lung, and Blood Institute, "Who Gets Sickle Cell Anemia?" September 2003, <http://www.nhlbi.nih.gov/health/dci/Diseases/Sca/SCA_WhoIsAtRisk.html> (March 28, 2005).

3. March of Dimes, "Sickle Cell Disease," *Quick Reference and Fact Sheets*, © 2005, <http://www.

marchofdimes.com/professionals/14332_1221.asp>
(May 2, 2005).

Chapter 4. Detection and Treatment

1. Adapted from: Olive Downer, "Caring for Arianne," *BBC—Birmingham Your Community*, July 2004, <http://www.bbc.co.uk/birmingham/your_community/2004/07/oscar/caring_for_arianne.shtml> (May 2, 2005).

2. Medical College of Wisconsin, "Alumna Profile - Betty S. Pace, MD '81, GME '84," *Alumni News*, Winter 2004, <http://www.mcw.edu/display/router.asp?docid =3770> (September 9, 2005).

3. Arlene McKanic, "A Look at Sickle Cell Anemia," *AOL Black Voices*, America Online © 2005, <http://bv.channel.aol.com/lifemain/health/sicklecell321> (September 8, 2005).

4. Laura Jana, M.D., "The Lifespan for a Person with Sickle Cell Disease," *Ask Dr. Jana*, February 28, 2001, <http://www.drspock.com/faq.0,1511,1720,00.html> (September 8, 2005).

5. Lab Tests Online, "Sickle Cell: The Test," *American Association for Clinical Chemistry*, modified November 15, 2001, <http://www.labtestsonline.org/understanding/analytes/sickle/test.html> (May 4, 2005).

6. University of Maryland Medical Center, "Sickle-Cell Disease—UMMC," reviewed December 21, 2002, <http://www.umm.edu/patiented/articles/what_treatments_aimed_at_sickle-cell_disease_itself_000058_7.htm> (May 5, 2005).

Chapter 5. Prevention

1. Philadelphia Eagles, "#81 Terrell Owens," *Official Web Site of the Philadelphia Eagles 2004 NFC Champions*, © 2005, <http://www.philadelphiaeagles.com/team/teamRosterDetails.jsp?id=9949> (May 10, 2005).

2. Mike Falcon, "Terrell Owens makes big play against sickle cell," *USA TODAY.com*, September 7, 2001, <http://www.usatoday.com/news/health/spotlight/2001-09-07-owens-sickle-cell.htm> (March 31, 2005).

3. Michael Miles, "Sickle Cell Disease Awareness Stamp to Be Issued by U.S. Postal Service: Stamp Design Highlights Need for Early Testing," *United States Postal Service*, August 27, 2004, <http://www.usps.com/communications/news/stamps/2004/sr04_059.htm> (April 6, 2005).

4. National Institutes of Health, National Heart, Lung, and Blood Institute, "Sickle Cell Research for Treatment and Cure," September 2002, <http://www.nhlbi.nih.gov/resources/docs/scd30/scd30.pdf> (May 11, 2005).

5. Ibid.

6. Doris L. Wethers, M.D., "Sickle Cell Disease in Childhood: Part I. Laboratory Diagnosis, Pathophysiology and Health Maintenance," *American Family Physician*, September 1, 2000, <http://www.aafp.org/afp/20000901/1013.html> (May 11, 2005).

7. Health Canada, Applied Research and Analysis Directorate, "Selected Legal Issues in Genetic Testing: Guidance from Human Rights. IV. Case Study on Testing in the Workplace: Health, Privacy and Discrimination," updated July 22, 2004, <http://www.hc-sc.gc.ca/iacb-dgiac/arad-draa/english/rmdd/wpapers/jones2.html> (May 16, 2005).

8. Tionne Watkins, *Thoughts* (New York: HarperEntertainment, 1999), p. 107.

Chapter 6. Sickle Cell Anemia and the Future

1. Frederic Golden, "The Sickle Cell Kid," *Time*, December 20, 1999, <http://www.defiers.com/cordbld.html> (March 31, 2005).

2. "Patients & Outcomes: Keone Penn," *National Cord Blood Program*, © 2003–2004, modified March 14, 2005, <http://www.nationalcordbloodprogram.org/patients/patient_keone.html> (March 31, 2005).

3. Bob Dart, "A voice of hope rings out in Senate; Lifesaving cure: Snellville teenager tells how cord blood cells ended sickle cell battle," *Atlanta Journal-Constitution*, June 13, 2003, p. 1E.

4. Cheryl A. Hiller, "The chicken or the egg? Tissue factor and inflammation in sickle cell disease," *Blood*, August 2004, pp. 595–596.

5. National Heart, Lung, and Blood Institute, "Sickle Cell Research for Treatment and Cure," *NIH Publication No. 02-5214*, September 2002, <http://www.nhlbi.nih.gov/resourcesdocs/scd30/scd30.pdf> (May 11, 2005).

6. "Sickle Cell Disease; Scientists identify sticky protein in sickle cell red blood cells," *Blood Weekly*, November 4, 2004, p. 137.

7. "Nitric Oxide Gas May Treat, Prevent Sickle Cell Crisis," *Doctor's Guide*, September 4, 1997, <http://www.pslgroup.com/dg/36776.htm> (May 16, 2005).

8. "New understanding of the causes for symptoms of sickle cell disease," *Medical Research News*, Duke University, January 31, 2005, <http://www.news-medical.net/?id=7592> (May 16, 2005).; Alan Schechter et al., "Key Gender Difference Found in Sickle Cell Disease," American Heart Association, December 26, 2002, <http://www.sciencedaily.com/releases/2002/12/021226071057.htm> (May 6, 2005).

9. Nathan Seppa, "Gene Therapy for Sickle-Cell Disease?" *Science News*, December 15, 2001, p. 372.

10. David M. Bodine, "Gene therapy for sickle cell disease marches on," *Blood*, December 15, 2003, p. 4247.

11. Laura Fraser, "PopSci's 2nd Annual Brilliant 10: Betty Pace, Molecular Medicine: University of Texas, Dallas: Unlocking genetic on/off switches to fool the body into healing itself," *Popular Science*, September 2003, p. 90; Medical College of Wisconsin, "Alumna Profile - Betty S. Pace, MD '81, GME '84," *Alumni News*, Winter 2004, <http://www.mcw.edu/display/router.asp?docid=3770> (April 4, 2005).

Glossary

amino acids—The chemical building blocks of proteins.

anemia—A condition in which the number of red blood cells (or the amount of hemoglobin) is below normal and is not enough to support the body's oxygen needs.

antibodies—Proteins produced by white blood cells that recognize and attack "foreign" chemicals, including those on the outer surface of bacteria, on cells that have been infected by viruses, and on cancer cells.

antigen—A chemical that stimulates antibody production.

artery (arteries _pl._)—A blood vessel that carries blood away from the heart to any part of the body.

blood vessels—Tubes that carry blood between the heart and all parts of the body.

bone marrow—Substance inside the cavities of bones that contains blood-forming cells.

capillary—A tiny, thin-walled blood vessel connecting an artery with a vein.

carrier—A person who is infected by a disease germ or has a gene for a hereditary disorder, but does not have any symptoms.

chromosomes—Structures inside each cell that contain the genes, coded in the form of DNA.

chronic—Lasting for years or possibly a lifetime.

circulatory system—The heart and the network of blood vessels (arteries, veins, and capillaries) that deliver blood to all parts of the body.

DNA (deoxyribonucleic acid)—The chemical of heredity, containing coded instructions for making body proteins.

dominant trait—A hereditary characteristic that is expressed even if the person has inherited the gene for it from only one parent.

electrophoresis—A technique for separating closely related chemicals according to how they move on a gel-coated slide or other surface in an electric field.

fetal hemoglobin—The main form of hemoglobin in the blood before birth and for a short time after birth.

folic acid—An important B vitamin needed for the production of red blood cells.

genes—Chemical units that determine hereditary traits passed on from one generation to the next.

genetic counseling—A program of testing, compiling family histories, and determining potential risks to help a couple make family planning decisions.

gene therapy—The transfer of normal (or genetically modified) genes to correct a hereditary disorder.

hand-foot syndrome—Painful redness and swelling of the hands and feet in children with sickle cell anemia.

hemoglobin—A red pigment in red blood cells that carries oxygen or carbon dioxide. Its molecule is made up of protein chains (globins) and a central iron-containing substance, heme.

hydroxyurea—A drug that stimulates increased production of fetal hemoglobin, which can prevent sickling.

immune system—The body's disease-fighting system, which includes the white blood cells.

inflammation—Swelling, pain, heat, and redness in the tissues around a site of infection.

inherited—Passed on by genes from parents to children.

jaundice—A yellowing of the skin and whites of the eyes; a sign of a blood or liver disorder.

malaria—A disease caused by a microscopic parasite, spread by mosquito bites. It is common in tropical regions of the world, such as much of Africa, the Mediterranean region, and the Caribbean.

recessive trait—A hereditary characteristic whose effects can be observed only if the person has inherited genes for it from both parents.

screening—Testing of large groups of people for a particular disease.

sickle cell—A red blood cell containing an abnormal form of hemoglobin, which changes to a crescent or sickle shape under low-oxygen conditions.

sickle cell crisis—An episode of intense pain that may require hospitalization.

sickle cell trait—The condition of carrying one gene for sickle cell disease. Usually people with the trait do not have any symptoms of illness.

sickling—The change of a red blood cell from its usual round, doughnutlike shape to a stiff crescent (sickle) shape.

stem cells—Immature cells that have the potential of developing into any type of cells or tissues.

stroke—Cutoff of the blood supply to a part of the brain, resulting in death of brain cells and loss of speech or other functions.

thalassemia—A blood disorder in which one of the types of hemoglobin chains is defective. Not enough hemoglobin is produced (resulting in anemia) and the unaffected chain builds up in excess in the blood.

thalassemia major—The most severe form of thalassemia; also called Cooley's anemia.

vein—A blood vessel that carries blood toward the heart.

Further Reading

Gillie, Oliver. *Just the Facts: Sickle Cell Disease*. Chicago, Ill.: Heinemann Library, 2004.

Gold, Susan Dudley. *Sickle Cell Disease*. Berkeley Heights, N.J.: Enslow Publishers, Inc., 2001.

Harris, Jacqueline L. *Sickle Cell Disease*. Brookfield, Conn.: Twenty-First Century Books, 2001.

Murphy, Wendy. *Orphan Diseases: New Hope for Rare Medical Conditions*. Brookfield, Conn.: Twenty-First Century Books, 2002.

Platt, Allan F., and Alan Sacerdote. *Hope and Destiny: The Patient's and Parent's Guide to Sickle Cell Disease and Sickle Cell Trait*. Roscoe, Ill.: Hilton Publishing Company, 2002.

Watkins, Tionne. *Thoughts*. New York: Harper Entertainment, 1999.

Internet Addresses

(See also **For More Information**, p. 96)

National Library of Medicine and the National
Institutes of Health. *Medline Plus*. "Sickle Cell
Anemia." <http://www.nlm.nih.gov/medlineplus/
sicklecellanemia.html>.

The Nemours Foundation. *Teens Health*. "Sickle Cell
Anemia." © 1995–2006. <http://kidshealth.org/teen/
diseases_conditions/genetic/sickle_cell_anemia.
html>.

Index

liver, 34, 45, 56, 79
lungs, 29, 32, 33, 34, 39, 42

M

malaria, 21
Mason, Verne, 19
Mediterranean, 7, 13, 43
meningitis, 41
Middle East, 7, 43, 44
mismatched blood, 58
mosquitoes, **21**
mouse experiments, 82, 87, 89

N

National Institutes of Health
  (NIH), 64
newborn screening, 7, 64–**66**
nitric oxide, 84–85
Noel, Walter Clement, 14–18

O

odds of inheriting sickle cell,
  70
Owens, Terrell, 61–63, **62**
oxygen, 22, 29, 31, 33–39, 51,
  73, 74, 85, 91, 92
oxygen and sickling, 21
oxygen mask, 10

P

Pace, Betty, **88**
pain, 7, 10, 22, 26, 36, 38, 39,
  48
pain crises, 12, 20, 26, 38–39,
  48, 91
    control, 54–59
    prevention, 70–76
    triggers, 75–76
pale skin, 45

Pauling, Linus, 21–**23**, 52
penicillin, 7, 65, 67, 93
Penn, Keone, 77–80, **79**
placenta, 80
plasma, 32–33
platelets, 32, 33, 51
pneumococcal pneumonia, 67
pneumonia, 7, 41, 73, 93
    vaccination, 7, 67
poor blood circulation, 42
Portugal, 13
positive attitude, 10

R

recessive genes, 32
red blood cells, 7, 10–**11**, 12,
  16, 18, **20**–22, 28–32, 34–**35**,
  36–37, 43, 50, 55–59, 83
reproductive organs, 11
rest, 50, 54, 71
Rubinstein, Pablo, **79**

S

Saudi Arabia, 13
sickle cells, 7, 18, **20**, 28, 36–37,
  56, 71
sickle cell anemia, 19
    cause, 7, 30
    diagnosis, 51–54
    symptoms, 7, 16, 38–43,
      44
Sickle Cell Disease Association
  of America (SCDAA), 10, 63
Sickle Cell Disease Awareness
  postage stamp, **63**
Sickle Cell Foundation, 62, 63
sickle cell screening, 7, 64–67,
  66, 68